NORDIC ACCORDION

NORDIC ACCORDION

POEMS IN A
SCANDINAVIAN MOOD

Bart Sutter

NODIN PRESS

ISBN: 978-1-947237-04-9
Design: John Toren
Cover photos: Dennis O'Conner (foreground) John Toren (background)
Author photo: Shawna Vine
Special thanks to Art Bjorngjeld (pictured on the cover)

Library of Congress Cataloging-in-Publication Data

Names: Sutter, Barton, 1949 - author.
Title: Nordic accordion : poems in a Scandinavian mood / by Bart Sutter.
Description: Minneapolis, MN : Nodin Press, [2018]
Identifiers: LCCN 2018003924 | ISBN 9781947237049
Classification: LCC PS3569.U87 A6 2018 | DDC 811/.54—dc23
LC record available at https://lccn.loc.gov/2018003924

Nodin Press
5114 Cedar Lake Road
Minneapolis, MN 55416
www.nodinpress.com

Printed in USA

For my brother Ross,
who kept the songs alive

Contents

I

The Immigrants:
A Story by Tom McGrath

Have you heard the parable that Tom McGrath,
Who felt at home beneath Dakota skies,
Worked up to tell us why we're still so lost?

Norwegians in their canvas-covered wagon
Creak across the endless prairie grass
When suddenly Lakota braves
Appear like distant birds along the skyline
Far behind them. Worried, Pa whips up
The horses, but the birds are ponies closing
Fast. The wagon's way too slow, and so
The family dumps the pedal organ off
The back; there goes the sacred music from
The last three hundred years. Still too much weight,
But who needs Shakespeare in translation here?
The *Edda* also goes. And Ibsen's too
Newfangled anyhow. They're rolling now,
The sweaty horses flecked with foam, but still
The braves are closing, so the Norskis chuck
The chest with all the porcelain. Kersmash!
No more fancy dinners now. They fling
The Bible, too. All those thees and thous.
The wagon shakes, about to fly apart,
The Indians are fading, but the quickest
Still persist, and Ma can see their faces
Streaked with paint. The children help her push
Poor Grandma out the back, and there she goes,

Cartwheeling through the sky. *Farväl, mormor!*
They crest the hill and shudder, jounce along,
The wagon empty, having ditched the braves,
And rattle on another day, arriving, finally,
At their claim of New World dirt and grass,
No history to burden them and nothing in their hands.

That's the myth McGrath made up to say
Why, even though we're fat from stolen land,
We know somehow we're missing something,
Something thrown away, and everything
We've worked so hard to win feels thin as dust
The next ferocious wind will blow away.

Wheelbarrow Man

So there was this fella who come out
To North Dakota, see, and he was a Norwegian.
This was all Indian Territory then,
And he was one of the first ones in.
They was awful hungry for land,
Them Scandihoovians,
And by the time that he got out here,
He didn't have much to work with,
And he was all alone. So he dug a hole
In the bank of the Sheyenne River here,
And he made a house of that.
Of course he damn near froze,
But he trapped along the river all that winter long—
Weasel, beaver, mink, and muskrat, maybe
A couple of skunks, and he stretched the skins.
Come spring, he piled his wheelbarrow high
With furs and walked his wheelbarrow
All the way to Fargo. How far is that? Over
A hundred miles! Think of that. That
Tickles me to think of that. So he sells his fur,
And he's pretty enthusiastic, he talks it up,
This country here by Devils Lake, what
The Indians called Spirit Lake, and isn't that
A difference interesting to think about?
So anyhoo, when he come back in summer,
There's a bunch of Norskis with him,
And they got a yoke of ox. Well,
That fella, he turned out over time to be

One of the richest guys around,
And it started with just a hole, a hole
He dug in the riverbank like he was
Some kind of badger, a badger
Who happened to own
A wheelbarrow, don't you know,
And isn't that just the way it goes?

Mina Anderson Contradicts
the Author Vilhelm Moberg

I had no dog years in America,
The way some say they did. An uncle who
Had gone before sent money for my crossing,
And I'm glad to say that I was able
To repay him that same year, because he died.
This was in Wisconsin, where I found
A good position working as a maid
For Swedes, a family I could understand.
Then I found another place to force
Myself to use the language here. They had
A little boy. I learned so much from him!
This was in a smaller town, but now
That I knew English, I could take the train
To Minneapolis-St. Paul and look
For higher pay. I found work easily
For more than double what I would have earned
In Sweden—cooking, cleaning, looking after
Children . . . but not one cow to milk!

In Sweden we worked twelve to sixteen hours
Every day. Here I had my evenings free,
So I went dancing with my friends. Such fun!
We bought fancy feathered hats and had
Our pictures taken for the folks back home,
Where only wealthy women went around
In hats. Soon, I met my husband, a kind
And decent man I learned to love. We
Bought land and made a farm. It wasn't easy.

We were first to homestead in this area,
So there wasn't even any road!
We had to walk out through the wild woods,
And it was thick with brambles. I nearly cried,
But then I spied a patch of strawberries,
So we sat down and ate. My spirits lifted,
And we found the spot where men were building
On our cabin. This was home. It almost
Burned that first year when the forest fires
Were so bad and my husband was away.
I saw it coming, but the wind was right,
And so I wet a gunny sack and set
A backfire. I beat my fire out around
The cabin. When my fire rushed and met
The forest fire, flames exploded fifty feet
And died. So I was proud. I saved our place.
I'd seen them do that back in Sweden. Then
I planted in the ash the summer after, and
Never did I see potatoes of such size.

My husband traveled in the spring and fall
In his profession as a tailor, so
I was somewhat lonesome till I thought
To take in boarders, decent Swedish men
Who were building their own homes, and when
Their people came, I had good neighbors. Soon
My boys were big enough to help with chores.
Worried they might drown in Bogus Brook,
I scared them with horrendous tales
Of Näcken, the Swedish water spirit, who

Might steal them if they went too close, but once
They'd gotten old enough to disbelieve,
They all could swim, and I had lost my fear.

I learned to drive a horse and do it all.
We slowly built the farm. We had neighbors
All around, and then, eventually, a school.
Young people came for dancing at our house,
But when we lost our William in the accident,
I could not bear to look at young folks
For some time. I have been a cheerful person,
But life will bring raw sorrow for anyone
Of woman born, and we must bear it as we can.

I've enjoyed my life here close to nature
And my neighbors, with a man who cared for me.
I was never like Kristina in that novel
Vilhem Moberg wrote, always pining
For the fatherland. Nor were any
Of the women that I knew who
Came over here as girls. Naturally,
I would have liked to visit that one stream
And certain berry bushes and a shade tree
Who were such good friends of mine when I was young.
But I never had regrets for leaving Sweden,
Where I was poor and had to work so hard.
This was better. Life was better here.
I had no dog years in America.

Halvor Halvorson

Here's to Halvor Halvorson,
    The Swedish boy who escaped
His foster folks and, on his own,
    Slipped aboard a ship.

Sailing out from Göteborg,
    He breathed the clean salt breeze.
Farväl to the mire of manure,
    The claustrophobic trees.

Halvor sailed the world around,
    Beyond his fantasies.
He watched a fellow sailor drown.
    He learned some Japanese.

He heard a superb soprano sing,
    The jungle squawk and howl,
The growl and groan of rigging
    When the weather turned foul.

But edging up to middle age
    And wanting something safe,
Halvor signed, for a decent wage,
To work the Great Lakes

On the last commercial sloop to sail
    The broad freshwater seas.
Bad luck when pelting rain and hail
    Blew up. The gale increased.

A wave washed Halvor overboard
  In boiling seas. No hope . . .
But, flailing, Halvor reached out for
  And grabbed a trailing rope.

He took a job at a new resort
  Down shore from Grand Marais,
And he had cause to thank the Lord
  Because he earned his pay

By rowing out a little skiff
  To pluck trout from the nets,
Well sheltered by the granite cliffs,
  With time for cigarettes.

By noon, he'd have his catch laid out
  Before him on the lawn
And crank the old victrola loud.
  He got that from the lodge.

Halvor conducted, knife in hand,
  As heartsick music played
And gulls whirled round but didn't land,
  Their wings like silver blades.

His knife would snick and slit the fish,
  And he'd strip out the offal.
The guests would hush each other, hiss:
  "Is that Italian opera?"

A powerful, pure soprano
    Filled the pine-sweet air:
O mio babbino caro . . .
    They wondered where they were.

A Nice Little Tavern in the Woods

for Jack Hickerson

You talk about
Your ethnic animosity,
There was a guy—
This was when I was a kid—
Was a Finnish guy
Had a nice little tavern
Back here in the woods—
Just off the curve,
Right back in here—
And he was a Finn,
A Finnish guy,
And he was death on Russians.

You go into his bar—
Nice little bar,
Log cabin place—
And order a vodka,
He'd throw you out.

Beyond belief, I know,
But that's the truth, that's it:
You go into his bar
Wearing anything red,
He'd throw you out:
"Out! Get out!" he'd shout.
"No Russians allowed!
Goddamn Commie bastards!"

We laugh about it now,
But I don't know, but
Maybe he'd lived in Karelia,
Maybe they took his family's land.
Maybe they killed his cousins.
World War II, you know.

That Finnish guy.
"Out! Get out!"
Lots of innocent folks were surprised.
Remember how they used to wear red
Instead of orange
In deer season?
His business didn't do too well
In deer season back then.

I Come from Quiet People

I come from quiet people—
Norwegians, Swedes, and Danes. Oh, sure,
Women gossiped in the clash
Of silverware and dishes,
Cleaning up, and children might
Shout their happiness at finding frogs
Or scream at fingers pinched in doors.
I guess there was a man or two
Who liked to talk and joke—
Arden Bergan digging graves,
Ruddy-faced and sweaty, he was funny,
But a drainage ditch fell in on him,
So he went quiet years ago.

It helped to have a talker at a funeral
Or a wedding, but how many do you need?
The preacher made pronouncements
From the pulpit every Sunday, but
He was paid for that, then, wasn't he?
The men who shook his hand
When he stopped talking
Gathered in the furnace room
Or on the steps outside,
The smoke from cigarettes
Ascending into heaven like
The ghost of speculation held in check.

Politics might get them going,
The closing of a creamery,
But big talkers were considered
Entertainment, like the radio
Or clowns cavorting at the county fair.

What mattered there was showing up
When hay was down and skies were turning black.
What happened when a farmer fell into his silo
And drowned in all that grain
He'd worked so hard to store?
Would you dare to tell his widow you were sorry?
Better to come bearing casseroles
Like crucibles of frankincense and myrrh.

A white pine doesn't have too much to say,
And deer just gaze or bound away.
Rivers remember the ocean, but
They don't brag about it much
And only roar a couple times a year.
Have you noticed how the aspens quake
And natter nervously when clouds go sickly green?
Yet all their chatter never changed
The course of a tornado.

Here now, the Tingelstads
Just lost their farm and have to move to town.
What say you lift the far end of that table there?
Let's see if we can't hoist her in their truck.

Funeral Rites

He met her at a funeral.
   It might have been a dance
Had they been younger. They were not.
   Despite the circumstance,

He couldn't help but notice her
   And thought he'd take a chance.
At the post-interment basement lunch,
   He gave her his best glance.

Her face was wrinkled, sure enough,
   But also soft and smooth.
She had a low and gentle voice
   Like mothers use to soothe.

He told a story on their friend.
   She laughed, and he rejoiced.
This woman might be past her prime
   But definitely choice.

Turned out she was Norwegian. Just
   Like his, her eyes were blue,
And what a wild coincidence—
   She liked coffee, too!

He felt his Else wouldn't mind;
   Her passing had been long
Ago. Now this pretty woman
   Was affecting him like song.

She had nice manners, liked to laugh
    But kept it dignified
And decent, as a person should,
    Their good friend having died.

They walked out to the parking lot.
    He asked if he might call
Someday to take her out for pie.
    She wasn't shy at all.

So that was the beginning there.
    He'd found his second wife.
He met her at a funeral
    That brought him back to life.

What Happened After the *Kumla* Was Served

At the Norwegian-American family Ufda Fest,
After the prayer in the grandmother tongue,
After the *kumla*, sauced with drawn butter,
The *kringla*, the fruit soup, the *krumkake*—
A sweet so fragile it shatters in your hand—
Followed by coffee and hymns in the language
Of lost mountains, glaciers, and fjords,
One son-in-law—a mongrel mix
Of German, French, and God knows what—
Was heard to grumble, "I think this ethnic
Stuff is overdone. We're all Americans now,
For chrissake!"

To which his Norski brother-in-law
Replied, "I see."

—A phrase which,
Translated from the Midwestern,
A highly cryptic dialect,
Means: "I hear you but might not agree.
Maybe, maybe not. Probably not.
I'll have to think about this thought
That you've expressed so recklessly
A dozen times or more
Before I get back to you,
Which I probably won't.
You are free

To think what you like
And act accordingly,
But, as for me and my house,
We are still awfully fond
Of the *respakaka*."

II

Tussocks

Right here on the edge
Of memory and everything
That matters most,
My father leads me from
His father's house, where
Old people speak Swedish
I can't understand, and
Here we go, in gloves and woolen jackets,
Up the hill and slanting down
Across the stubble hayfield
Into trees and through
The spooky woods, emerging
At the marsh. Ducks
Explode from yellow grass
And startle me. They fly away,
And everything grows quiet
Once again, more silent
Than before. *Quack.*
Quiet, quiet, quiet—*quack,*
A fading sound, far off.

And now my father says
We're going to cross the marsh.
But how? There's water,
Splinterings of ice.
He points out
Bumpy lumps of grass,
Like little islands.

These are tussocks.
You jump from hump
To hump, and so
We hopscotch
Cross the marsh,
Frightening and fun.
Towards the end,
I slip. Icy water
Sucks my foot.
My father grabs my hand
And swings me to the land.

We climb a grassy rise
And stretch out, warmed
By morning sun, bare branches
High above. He tells me
How he came here as a boy
With brothers, who are uncles
Now that I'm the boy,
And one of them is dead (the war),
To watch the wildlife below.
And there! A flock of wood ducks,
Extravagantly colored, coast
Back home and curl the water as they land.
Years from now, I'll find
His penny notebook with the drawings—
Duck and mink and rabbit—
And excited scribbling, drifting smoke
Of how the turning seasons
Burned with meaning then.

I don't know too much
This morning on the hillside
Since I'm only four or five.
It will be half a century
Before I learn third-hand
That just a few years earlier
My father woke to find his friend
In the foxhole next to his
Hacked to pieces in the night,
Reported that attack, then joined—
This peaceable and loving man—
His captain's group
Of volunteers who hunted
Down that Japanese patrol
And killed them, every one.

The world is full of dangers,
But I'm ignorant this morning,
And we've crossed the swampy spot
On tussocks, as I'll cross the world
Throughout my days, remembering,
Deep down, beneath awareness,
How to find this sunshot hillside
Where a faint perfume of woodsmoke
Drifts like incense on the wind
And my father snugs me to his side.

Birgit and Guri

Birgit and Guri. Norwegian, no doubt,
Or Danish, perhaps. I can't really say.
My memory's dim, and I can't figure out
Why spinsters moved into my mind to stay.

Though they sound like the daughters of Thor,
Birgit and Guri survived on a farm
When I was a pipsqueak way up north,
Two tidy sisters with no special charms.

Birgit and Guri were kindly but dull.
In the kitchen, they spoke with my folks about God
And served cream and bread till I was plumb full.
With no kids around, it was boring and odd.

Their house was so silent you heard yourself think.
Sunlight polished the hardwood floors.
At the end of the hall stood an immigrant's trunk.
A spinning wheel perched by the living room door.

They keep floating up from the depths of nowhere
Like a long-forgotten vaudeville team
Or a highly promising ice-skating pair
Who never earned more than local fame.

They sound like they could be a trendy shop,
But Birgit and Guri keep gazing at me,
Two shriveled women who will not be mocked,
Persisting in quiet dignity.

There's no reason at all to recall those old dames
Who withered and died in the last century,
But they are determined I tell you their names:
Birgit. And Guri. Birgit and Guri.

Strange Doings at Ross Elementary, 1956

When I was a kid on the Canadian border,
The grade school in the village there was plural—
Schools—because the farm folks roundabout
Had simply hauled in clapboard houses
On their flatbed trucks, set them on foundations
In a field, and hired teachers. Each teacher
Taught two grades, two grades per house,
Grades one through six, with one house left
To serve as cafeteria. They built a rink
With warming house, and, bingo, problem solved.

Everything was painted white because
The winters were so long no one could think
In any other color. The teachers helped us
Lace our skates for recess and called us
Back to work by standing on their porches
Swinging bells. Sometime along in May,
When ice had finally melted in the rink,
We cut rubber band boats out of plywood
And sent them puttering across the muddy ocean.

There were strange doings at that school. One day,
A classmate brought a flag for show-and-tell:
Scarlet, with a blue-and-white cross on its side.
This was the flag of Norway, and he'd fashioned it
To show that he was more than just American,
He was Norwegian, too. That flag inflamed us,
Made us crazed with jealousy, and we

Spent every recess chasing him while Norway
Fluttered in the wind he made by running wild.
That night, our houses stayed up late,
Brightened by the sound of bed sheets
Ripping and our humming as we colored them
And tacked the colors onto strips of lath.

Next day, the cloakroom bristled with our standards:
The red-and-white of Denmark, the sun-and-sky of Sweden,
The sky-and-snow of Finland, and Germany was there,
And Iceland looked like Norway inside out. At recess,
First and second graders of Ross Elementary
Burst from the schoolhouse like patriotic banshees
In high-speed parade, flags rippling in the breeze,
As we snaked around the schoolyard, ran
Full tilt, ecstatic, tears streaking from our eyes
Because the wind, because our grandparents,
Because we were carried away by who knows what.
A fundamental lesson in geography,
Phys. Ed., war, and just plain odd behavior
Which has lasted me my whole life long.

Grand Casino

at my grandparents' grave

I park beneath the gnarled locust tree—
A welcome break, halfway to the city—
And lift the hard cardboard vase free
Of the seatbelt, thinking: Cheap. Still pretty.
Then say aloud: "I've brought you these fake flowers."
I place them in the little graveside cage,
Where they will slowly fade, whipped and scoured
As the sleet storms and the blizzards rage.

I like to read the flat, smooth stones:
Esther, born in 1894,
And John, who lived his final days alone
And died a quarter century before
She eased in here beside him. She was plain,
Big-boned and sturdy, but she wanted him
And won him with flirtatiousness and girlish games,
This boy who looked so dangerously handsome

The day he came to plough her family's garden.
The earth turned over as he held the reins
Of that huge horse. Her desire hardened,
And eventually they married, half insane
With foggy dreams of middle-class glory.
She wanted a bungalow with a white picket fence,
But he, poor fellow, longed to be somebody,
He and a million other immigrants.

An affable man, he had a gift for sales
And sold himself on many things: windows,
Pots and pans, a gas station that failed
For not collecting money he was owed.
"They *loved* him at the hardware store,"
Esther said in later years. "He should
Have stuck with that. The pay was rather poor,
But it was steady. He thought he was too good

"For that, so he went chasing something else.
Then we got caught, of course, by the Depression."
And even he could see his dreams were false.
Handyman, gypsy electrician,
He stole some juice to light the house on one
Cold Christmas. Saved by World War II.
Shipyard work. He could run a rivet gun
And hammering hot metal got them through,

Although it ruined his hearing, naturally.
Well, he's awfully hard of hearing now.
No point in yelling how he gradually
Destroyed his marriage, drinking, doubling down
On dreams, the sexy women he attracted.
When I faulted him one time, my aunt
Attacked: "You don't know the half of it—
Her pushiness, her carping, her demands."

And so they slowly pulled apart, although
Esther swore that John was a terrific father.
"I'll never complain about that." And this we know

From the loving testimony of his daughters.
But there was trouble, like the day the Spaniard
And his son both lay in wait with baseball bats.
Warned away, John skipped his shift at the shipyard
And took the family picnicking at Fond du Lac.

Approaching seventy, she'd had enough
And said so when she got back from a trip.
Done with sneaking, whiskey, lies, and snuff,
She stepped into the room, set down her grip,
And spoke the words she'd only thought before.
It was like a movie: Bogie and Bacall.
Surprised, he turned to ask her, "What's the score?"
She said, "Your life caught up with you, that's all."

But when he died, she saved his dignity,
Rescued him once more, to bury here,
Not unlike the time the Model T
Fell off the jack and she just lifted up the car
So he escaped without one broken bone.
She bought this plot, the one beside him, too,
And saved for years to buy these simple stones
To show their love, however false, was also true.

Not far from here, they've built a grand casino.
Don't we always bet? It's just a gamble
When we marry. There's so little we can know!
The dreams of these two ended in a shambles,
But who am I to judge? I've also stumbled
And can guess how hard they tried. And so
I bring bright flowers every fall and mumble
My affection, which means nothing to the snow.

Approaching Winter Solstice

Night. Night night.
Will we ever see the light
In each other's eyes again?
Or baseball? Or scarlet tanagers?
How much darkness
Can a person stand?

But let's not get depressed.
Let's rejoice in the suffering of others!
Think of Stina and her friends
Above the Arctic circle.
By now they're so terrified
Of light, they're down to candles,
Little lamps, fireflies in bottles
They saved since last July.
They'd rather just bumble around
In the dark, mumbling Norwegian,
Than suffer the predatory flash
And shock of a fluorescent light.
How could you ever recover
From that? When they dream,
They no longer dream
The harsh light of high noon
But the copper-colored water
And the foggy light at midnight
When they fish for cod in June.

Meantime, down in Sweden,
Down in Dalarna, Margit and Bosse,
Whose eyesight has grown dim
In any case because of age,
Can't see a thing this time of year,
So when they venture to the village
They must hold each other by the hand
As they go creaking through the snow.
Not that they much mind.
They dream the same dream, too:
Church boats cross the lake,
The snow has turned to cotton grass,
The birds are chattering,
And there's a moose!

Night. Night night. At least
The sun shows up around here
Now and then, like some sulky teenager
Who's only interested in food.
Where the hell have you been?
What are you doing all night?
Are you on drugs? You look so pale.

Should we be wearing headlamps
All day long? Are we miners underground?
And if we light this darkness,
Will it burn? I will not sacrifice
My daughter, but I'm thinking

I'd be willing to decapitate a squirrel
If that would bring some light
Into this murky world.

I do believe
That we might find enlightenment
If we went far enough,
Far up in the Orkney Islands,
If we crawled inside Maeshowe,
That ancient chambered tomb
With the usual human gibberish
Written there in Viking runes—
"Inge is most beautiful of all"—
And one telescope or gun sight opening
Through which, on the one day in December,
Light strikes, and the stone room blooms.

A Taste for Ptarmigan

On December first, it snowed a foot.
On the second, it snowed two more. Then
It quit and turned off cold, so
Cars refused to start and people just sat still.
Musk ox weather, day by day.
The nights were spooky, too. Boom!
You'd hear the ice crack on the lake
Or, worse, the rafters in your house.
Nails popped. The screws came loose.
You still had windows, but what could you see
With frost flowers grown fantastically opaque?

New Year's Day, it snowed an inch.
On the second, we got two. On the third,
Three inches more. I said to the wife,
"What's the use?" She passed the sugar bowl.
I sprinkled some over my flakes, repulsed because
The crystals fell like you-know-what, but
I needed the oomph to shovel the roof.
I got right down to shingles. That night, a blizzard hit.
Everywhere I looked looked white. Salt. Sheets.
The tablecloth. The fish in my *mojakka*.

Open the door, you'd close it quick: snowy owls
On the rooftops. Snow leopards in the streets.
Crows had fled the country, replaced by ptarmigan.
I grabbed the .410 and blasted one.
The oven still worked, so we seasoned the bird,

And I'll say this: It wasn't bad. Not bad at all.
Tasted a little like chicken, with a hint of juniper.

Our hair was turning white. The wife was
Fading, pale, her brown eyes going gray.
One morning, gazing down on her in bed,
I thought she looked so pitiful and snug,
I said, "You might as well stay in your drift."
I brewed her a cup of tea but didn't add any cream.
I brought it to her nice and hot . . . and dark
As garden earth we turn up in the spring.
She reached out a ghostly hand and said,
"Baby, come on inside."

She treated me so sweet that I saw fireworks
And lost all track of time. When I woke up,
The robins sang, and kids were playing catch.
Neighbors came to lunch on the lawn.
The wife was toasty brown. By nightfall, though,
I longed for a hockey game, and, leafing through
The calendar, I daydreamed flakes and drifts
And felt a strange affection for the ice cubes in my drink.

On Being Mistaken for Dan Carlson

So I'm coming out of the post office,
Having just mailed a letter to Denver,
And I'm marveling at this miracle
By means of which I can,
For the price of pocket change, transport
My signature to Anchorage or say hello
To Honolulu, although I've chosen Denver,
And I'm also pleased to think
However I may fail today,
I've done this bit of business, anyway,
And isn't it nice the ferocious cold has eased,
Though nobody would know it
To see me in my green wool coat
With collar up against the nonexistent wind
And my stocking cap yanked down around my ears,
When a friendly fellow says to me
Through the open window of his car,
"How ya doin', Danny?"

Which causes me to pause.

I do a double take, lean in, and say, "I'm afraid
You've taken me for someone else,"
Offering a hand to shake and telling him my name.
"Oh, shit," he laughs, ashamed,
"You look just like Dan Carlson."

"So I've got a twin I never knew," I grin
And turn away as he calls after me,
"Though Dan is better-looking!"

Driving off, I'm both delighted and disturbed
To know my lookalike is on the loose,
And that's just what's been wrong with me, I think.
All these years I thought I was so special!

Yet all along there's been this other me,
This Dan, Dan Carlson, who's worn my build,
My face—albeit handsomer. Maybe we could meet,
Trade clothes, cars, wives, think each other's thoughts,
And who would be the wiser?

Back home—at least I think I'm home—I check
The phone directory, discover, though the two of us
Are duplicates, half a dozen Daniel Carlsons
Occupy our town, and, curious as I am,
There's no damn way I'm going to phone
            six different Dans
To see if they believe they look at all like me,
And isn't it a pity, Dan, a shame, a sorry sin,
To think that now we'll never find out who we are
Or who we might have been.

III

Welcome to Iceland

Let's go hunt puffins, hard by the sea.
Let's get some puffins, just you and me.
Hand me that light rod, limber and long.
Hang onto my legs. Hold on real strong
When I lash at the air with my puffin net.
Don't let me drop. I don't want to get wet.
It's a thousand feet down from this clifftop,
And I would prefer not to flippety-flop.
We'll roast them in front of our turfy hut,
Which resembles a house in an old woodcut.
We'll have us some schnapps just to get loose.
Puffin tastes great. It's a lot like goose.
Let's go hunt puffins, hard by the sea.
Let's get some puffins, just you and me.

Let's lower you over the edge on a rope.
Whatever might happen, I know we can cope.
We'll give you this apron, fill it with grass
To cradle the eggs you snatch as you pass.
Puffin and fulmar, gannet and gull,
Their eggs are all tasty. Chickens' are dull.
But watch for the skua, who might well attack.
Here's a light racket. Just give him a whack.
Iceland's for heroes. Strangle your fear.
We've gathered cliff eggs for hundreds of years.
So here you go, over the edge on this rope.
Whatever might happen, I know we can cope.

Dagna Fahlstrom Fails to
Send a Postcard Home

When Dagna found herself at last
In Kalmar, the city on the Baltic
From which her grandmother had emigrated
As a girl, she was so excited that she bought
A dozen postcards, all the same
Picture of the castle, which delighted her
It looked so like a medieval hat.
Imagine that—a castle! Which could have been hers,
Kind of, if her grandmother had just stayed put.
Dagna indulged a daydream, briefly,
That she was banished royalty
Before she told herself, *Enough of that!*
And, ordering a *kaffe* from the cafe,
Found herself a table by the window
That opened on the sea. Think of it—
The sea! There it was, crashing on the sand.

Dagna dug the ballpoint from her purse,
The little red address book that contained
Her relatives and friends in Minnesota,
Overturned a postcard . . . but she had so much to say
She couldn't start. To tell the truth,
She'd been fascinated by the dungeon
And peculiar forms of torture
To which transgressors were subjected long ago,
Proving that her ancestors were really not so nice,
And she guessed she wasn't, either,

With her interest in such things. But
She could write about the Baltic,
The brightly painted houses Minnesotans
Would condemn as "gaudy," though they'd like
The way the flowerboxes overflowed with color,
And the clothes the women wore, so simple,
Rich, and tempting—tweedy, nubby, creamy—
She could hardly stay her hand
When they walked by, and then
The handsome man who'd gazed at her
So long in Stockholm she'd felt weak,
Not to mention all this funny money, so unreal
She was spending like a sailor come to port,
And, my goodness, Dagna understood
Quite suddenly, all of this would never fit
Within the limits of a postcard!
Besides, how would friends react,
Stuck back home in Detroit Lakes,
When her castle cards arrived
With their exotic stamps?

Oh, she knew how *she* had felt
When she'd received such cryptic missives
In her mailbox—first a little lift
To think a friend had thought of her
In the midst of an adventure overseas,
Followed by the icky burn of envy.

No. She would not hurt her friends like that.
Dagna looked down at the dozen

Medieval castles in her hand
And tapped them on the table
Like a deck of playing cards,
Ashamed of her extravagance.

Outside, the sea, the sky, the . . . everything
Was slowly growing dark. She slipped
The postcards in her purse and thought,
"I guess they'll work as bookmarks."

First Night on Sollerön

Ancestral memories brought me here,
  The dream in lilting words,
The homesick ache of kitchen talk.
  Small boy, I overheard.

Small boy, himself, my granddad left
  A century back and more,
Fared forth with family from Göteborg
  For the mist of America.

My family has the diary
  His father tried to write:
Three pages long, the story stops
  As Sweden sinks from sight.

Seasick, maybe. Or racked by doubts
  About his headstrong deed.
When he resumes, it's all mundane:
  The price of tools and seed.

We know what's missing in that book,
  The heave and toss, the wind,
The waves, the retching as they thought
  Of those they left behind.

The generations rose and fell,
  Our svenska flickered out,
But some old song insisted on
  The tickets that I bought.

We circle the lake by rental car
  And cross the causeway where
Dead men used to strain with oars.
  Prodigal son, I'm here,

Although I can't say why for sure.
  To somberly stroll the graveyard
And trace my last name carved in stone,
  The dream of home rock-hard?

We find our temporary house,
  Reserved for "cultural workers."
A welcome note, food in the fridge,
  Fish roe and knäckerbröd.

The living room has a fireplace
  With kindling set to light.
Upstairs, a porch looks everywhere,
  But I want second sight.

Why would anyone want to leave?
  We wonder as we walk
Beneath dark pines and glimmering birch,
  Then realize with a shock

Potatoes that cover a small field
  Can't be spuds. It's June.
And of course a closer look reveals
  No harvest but brown stones.

Back at the house, we murmur and snoop
    Where Margit and Suzanne
Have left their notes on the dialect
    In a dark blue hand.

The language of the old folks here
    Is vanishing, it seems,
Like bream that break beyond the net,
    Phosphorescent gleams.

After supper, I stroll alone
    Down to the village pier,
Where shadowy men have gathered to launch
    The dream they built this year:

A boat. A lightweight, lapstrake boat,
    Handmade, in Viking style,
From planks they steamed and slowly bent
    To form this buoyant smile.

The strakes were edged and overlapped,
    Rivets driven, clenched.
They planed and shaved long winter nights,
    And now it's time to launch.

Each in turn, they row the skiff
    To laughter, muffled shouts,
And then they ask the foreigner,
    Would I care to take her out?

It floats, the boat, like a memory,
    Deja-vu come true,
Swivels and glides in the dusky light,
    So buoyant, slippy-smooth.

"Oh, Grandfather," I want to cry,
    "We're whispers on the water."
But I know how to choke such thoughts,
    Don't want to be a bother.

Rowing backwards to the beach,
    I step from the waking dream,
With neither Swedish nor English words
    To venture what I mean.

I offer, "*Tack. Tusen tack!*"
    And leave them to their triumph,
Returning up the long, slow hill,
    Thrilled by the curlews crying.

The nights are white on Sollerön
    In June. They're gauzy, pale,
And we sleep lightly, wake and turn,
    The sheets like tangled sails.

Where have we traveled, love, and why?
    Once, in the night, we kissed.
At dawn, we wake to another dream:
    Dark horses in the mist.

What Swedes Eat

Flatbread, butter, fish eggs, jam,
Yogurt, filmjölk, cheese, and ham.

Hardboiled, softboiled, scrambled, fried.
Sunbright yolks diversified.

Rye bread, wheat bread, white, brown, black.
Sneak some for a midday snack.

Herring—sautéed, pickled, creamed.
Beets and turnips, salad greens.

Reindeer, beefsteak, pork roast, moose.
Have some gravy or *au jus*.

Haddock, salmon, sea bass, trout.
Pray the Baltic won't run out.

Crayfish, lobster, eelpout, cod.
Dill sauce, butter, oh my god.

Bacon, ham hocks, lamb, and goat.
Pancakes, pea soup, boiled oats.

Blueberries, lingonberries, cloudberries, straw.
Thanks to the meadows. *Tack ska du ha*.

Mushrooms, moss, mice, and bugs.
Thank the forest for your grub.

Birch bud soup, shoe leather stew.
Crickets glistening with dew.

Rock tripe, inner bark of pine.
Save us from starvation times.

What Happened Up in Uppsala

The Swedes have grown so rational
They won't be pleased to learn you know
What happened up in Uppsala
A thousand years ago or so.

The Swedes, of course, would sooner point
To their cathedral, long and tall,
Though they were rather late to join
The church and hardly go at all.

But just a couple miles north
Of town lies Gamla Uppsala,
Where once dark forces in the earth
Drew folk from all of Sverige.

Within their wooden temple there,
Encircled by a golden chain,
Thor, enthroned, held up his spear;
Freyr, his proud erection;

Odin, lord of all, his mace.
I wonder if it was taboo
To stare at such a statue's face.
I'd hesitate. Wouldn't you?

Odin, they said, had hanged himself
For nine long days to learn the things
He knew: foresight, poems, runes, and spells.
So here they came with offerings

Whenever nine more years had passed.
Oddly, their priests were called "the cooks."
But then ours feed us bread at mass
And raise a hand to wish us luck.

Each day nine animals were hanged.
A sheep, a goat, a horse, a man . . .
All male, all corpses left to dangle,
According to their pagan plan,

From branches in the sacred grove.
So by the time they reached day nine,
Many bodies proved their love
And loyalty to Odin.

Vultures, ravens came to feast
On carcasses half rotted
As the people prayed to ease
Their fears. They drank until besotted.

In the grove bonfires flickered
On the living and the dead. Singing
Rose like smoke. A vivid picture.
Can't you hear their voices ringing?

I guess we're out of earshot now.
Jesus, hung on Golgotha,
A god to whom the Swedes would bow,
Was close enough to Uppsala.

Today, they'll gladly show the way
To Uppsala Universitet,
Where students, on commencement day,
Wear leafy crowns and stovepipe hats.

But since we still can't guess our fate,
These days we buy insurance,
Pay tribute by a certain date,
Resentful, with no confidence.

Because we know we all must die—
Hard fact, which horrifies—
Because we suffer, clutch and cry,
Willy-nilly, faith must rise.

Or else, at funerals, we're keening
Over so much meat and fat.
Human life must have more meaning!
We insist on that.

And haven't you felt, once or twice,
How Something won't be satisfied
By aught but bloody sacrifice
And smoky torches in the night?

Cotton Grass

About the time trout start to bite, you might
Be driving the back roads or out for a hike
And stop at the sight of . . . what? . . .
Receding snow? Surveyor's flags?
Dozens of daisies? No. Fluffed by the breeze,
Cotton grass brightens the greening meadow
Edging the black spruce bog.

It's a sedge, not grass, but does not care
What you call it—ghost grass, wool grass,
White delight, dauber-on-stiff-stem,
Jittery-joy-of-this-June-day—
As a killdeer cries nearby.

Its root stalks like wet ground,
So the little white flags signal Danger.
Bog Warning. Back Off. Stay Clear.
Or you might get sucked out of sight
And turn to tar, sunk in ick-black peat.

What should you make of this
Modest beauty that circles the globe,
Contiguous with hardy tribes
Of the Circumpolar Bear Cult?
The fibers of cotton grass heads are too brittle
To spin into thread, but Swedes
Have stuffed pillows with ghost grass.
Imagine. Imagine their dreams.

Up in the Land of Dwarf Willow,
The Yupik have twisted them into candlewicks,
The Finns have used them as tinder,
Which takes the spark, which grows to flame,
The red wolf that drives off the dark.
Scots found wool grass will dress wounds.
Siberians swear that chewing the stem
Will dry up your diarreah.

These knee-high plant people stand
          their damp ground,
Their white flags flutter in place, so you think
They are stuck in the mud, but
They do move. Even now, right here,
As you watch, their anthem, the wind, is rising,
Their tufted seeds loosen and lift aloft
To ride the skies, and then, thanks
To their silken parachutes, softly, softly
Descend. Cotton grass circles the globe.

IV

Fäbod

We take the two-track road into the hills
With Margit and Suzanne. Something sacred
Here, a hush, with soft birdsong for bells.
Fäbod: a place where animals will dwell.
Sunlight floods the camp. Below, the island
And the lake recede, a galaxy in space.
We feel a gentle vertigo. Our guides
Are happy, shy, restrained. They murmur
When they speak. Three cabins, silver-gray
With age, low sheds, a storage house
On stilts. For centuries, island women
Brought their cows, boating them across,
Then climbed up here for summer grass.

I draw some water for the pot and then
Strip off my shirt to wash while dipping from
The wooden sluice. The women laugh and hoot
At my ablutions. It's an act, to entertain—
Grandson of Emigrants Returns to Mollify
The Ancestors—but don't I hope for absolution
Sort of? No? How about some coffee, then?

Coffee, yes. Margit serves, with sweets
For complements. We keep our conversation low
In dusky light, huddled here within
The silver, seasoned walls, where everything
Feels worn—benches, chairs, ladles, churns.
Every handle here was handled by the dead.

Long before my parents' folks were born,
Someone carved the year in that box bed.

We venture out along the ridge, and there
We sink among the mosses, breathing air
The pines have peppered, picking berries—
Blues and lingons—glad enough, although they say
These can't compare to cloudberries up north.

It's time. We rise, and, gazing out, Suzanne
Lets loose a cow call, freezing us in place:
A she-wolf howling for her mate, a wild cat
But far more musical, a yodel, alpenhorn,
Some whippoorwill, some loon, the yowling
      of an owl,
A bellowed moo, a sob, a cry. Oh, who
Can say? The wind is in it, too. It rises,
Then descends, unfurling down the sky,
But I get some before it goes. I breathe it in
And keep it, here, covered by my skin.

Helga Recites Instructions

Climbing to the *fäbod*,
  Be sure to cut a branch
And twist it counterclockwise
  Until you form a loop.
Once you've reached the cow camp,
  Lay it on the ground
And make yourself some *sletje*,
  Salt with flour, mixed.
Pour it in the circle.
  Reach with your right hand.
Offer some to every cow
  And put some in the bell.
Sleep with your best cowbell
  Three nights in a row.
No matter where the herd goes,
  If you have done this right,
All the scented summer long,
  They'll come home at night.

Alva Tells the Troll Dance

When I went up to cow camp—
   You talk about romance!—
We thundered on the floorboards,
   We did a noisy dance
To tell the trolls that we were back
   And they should disappear.
We only wanted summer grass.
   We wouldn't stay the year.

The cows all seemed to recognize
   The meadow right nearby;
We turned them loose, unsupervised.
   My neighbor showed where I
Should sleep and where I ought to fetch
   Our water from the spring.
The air was heady, fresh and rich,
   The world awakening.

Aunt Solvig warned me not to pour
   Hot water near a post
Or I might scald the little folk,
   Another kind of ghost.
I still can hear our boots go *bang*
   To drive the trolls away.
Oh, how we stomped and whooped and sang!
   They don't do that today.

Worksong

Up at four and out the door.
Tease Aunt Solvig. How she snored!
Churn the cream until it's butter.
Grab a bucket, wash the udders,
Milk, and let the cattle out,
Then turn to and go about
Your business, heating skim,
And don't forget, put rennet in.
You'll be in the woods all day,
So wash the buckets and the trays,
Clean the barn, and press the cheese.
Time for porridge. Take your ease.
Butter? Cream? More coffee, please.

Call the cows. Turn and go
Up the narrow cattle road
To forest meadows, grassy bogs
The cows can graze. Find a log
Where you can take your lunch and sew
On one of several shirts you owe.
Everywhere a cowgirl walks,
She'll be knitting pairs of socks,
Finding wood to fashion tools
Villagers below will use.
Listen for your leader's belltone;
Call the cows and sing them home.

Milk again and fix your meal,
Wash the dishes, tell a tale,
Lilt a tune or sing a hymn,
Relaxing as the light grows dim.

Their Instruments

Cowgirls used a range of tools
   Besides the human voice.
Their strongest weapon was the lur,
   A Swedish didgeridoo.

They'd huff and blow the lur to warn
   Their friends and frighten wolves.
It sounded like a sick foghorn,
   A grumbling thunderstorm.

Some carried birch bark megaphones,
   A kind of make-do lur,
To blow in an emergency.
   They called them screaming-horns.

Their willow flutes perfumed the air,
   But they were dangerous.
Played for pleasure, such sweet sounds
   Were sure to draw a bear.

Because they lived among the cows,
   They had, quite naturally,
Cow horns. Broken ones were best,
   But they were not allowed

For music in the house. Power
　　Could be lost indoors;
Magic might escape like smoke
　　Or wilt like tired flowers.

Lisa was told to tie her horn
　　Beneath her wedding dress,
And her cows always came for her.
　　Her horn grew smooth and worn.

Mountain Medicines

1.
My parents helped me clean our cabin,
   Showed me all I had to do.
I was just eleven then,
   So I was frightened blue
When they went down the mountain.

I had good neighbor ladies, though,
   Who saw I felt so awful sick
For home I could not eat, and, oh,
   They pulled a sneaky trick.
The sorcery they used to know!

They shaved some splinters off our door
   And slipped them in my coffee pot,
Then chuckled as they watched me pour.
   It worked, for I was not
The least bit homesick anymore.

2.
Once my favorite cow was bitten by a snake.
Her face swelled up like this, and I, myself, felt sick
With worry, not to mention sorry for her sake.

The neighbor women sent me skittering
Down the mountain trail—a long way to the village!
I absolutely had to find some medicine,

But nobody had anything! They said, "Go see the Finn!"
An old, dry-wrinkled man, he had some special cures,
And so I hurried up his way, praying he'd be in.

He was! He told me, "What you need is ermine meat.
Lucky you, I have some here. It's poisonous,
An antidote if you can get your cow to eat."

Once I made it back to camp, I was near worn out.
My cow was down and looked as if she wouldn't last.
I raised her head, somehow opened up her mouth.

Holding Rosie tight, I tipped the paper cone
The Finn had filled with dried, chopped ermine meat
And poured it down her throat. Rosie gave a groan

But stood. I snatched my stool so I could milk her dry
And work the antidote right through her big hot body.
Thanks to ermine meat, our best cow did not die.

Cow Calls in Dalarna

1.
There were many melodies in the forest
Up there on the mountainsides,
And cowgirls kept inventing them.
There was "C'boss!" of course, "Come home.
It's time to milk." There was "Here we go
Through the woods. Keep to the trail.
I promise you fresh grass." There was
"Damn it! Where are you cows, anyhow?"
And there was "There, there. There, there."

But cowgirls called each other, too,
Across the hills, from camp to camp.
"I've lost my cow." "We've found your cow."
"Watch out. There's a bear nearby."
"Why don't you come for coffee?"
"I'll meet you at the big rock."
These were the sorts of songs they sang.
And once in a while, one of them sang
Spontaneously, unpredictably,
She had no control whatsoever:
"What a magnificent morning!"

These songs had sex in them and dreams,
Pain and fear and love. They were beautiful
But wild and raw. It's a very good thing
There was no sea near, or many a ship
Would have wrecked on the rocks, the sailors

Insane with longing on hearing those songs.
They sounded like solo saxophones
In the mountains, floating like smoke
From the forest, down from the meadows and camps.

2.
We can lose ourselves in romantic fog
Recalling the sound of those songs,
But we must remember these people
Were tragically simple, so backward and slow
They could not conceive of aluminum foil
And moved through their lives unaware
Of something as useful as Tupperware.
They still fashioned baskets from bark
By hand. They walked everywhere and knit
Their own sweaters and socks, whereas
We can just drive to the store. They knew
Every one of their cows by name and drank
Unpasteurized milk! They were so superstitious
They thought that metal would ward off the devil,
While we have examined invisible atoms
And smashed them to pieces, too.

The oceans are choking, the glaciers are melting,
But that's a small price to pay
For computers and movies, I'm sure you agree.
We can telephone dozens of times a day,
But the cowgirls could only sing to each other
Across the green hillsides: "*Hello,*
Beware! Hello, beware!
This morning I saw a wolf!"

Those women, poor things, knew nothing
Of air-conditioning. They were often
Slippery with sweat. No doubt,
They smelled like women, like bread
And butter, cowhide, and earth, and not
The blend of eucalyptus and acetone
We tend to prefer today. What can we say
About women so plain that a berry patch
Could cause them to smile and sing?
They were ignorant. They were dumb,
Except, of course, for their songs, or else
Why did the last old men who remembered them weep,
Haunted by girlsong, ancient womanly melodies
Rising like columns of mist and drifting down the dales?

3.
Anthropologists caught
A few of those songs on tape
Toward the end of the cow call era,
Recording withered women at home.
To test for authenticity, they played them back
For another crone, who'd had her cowgirl years.
She laughed to hear "My cow is stuck in a bog!"
And then went dreamy and sad at the sound
Of "The boys are coming up tonight."
But when they played, "C'boss! Come home.
It's time to milk," she frowned and declared,
Conclusively, "That one isn't real." "Why not?"
The anthropologist asked. "How can you tell?"
"Plain as the nose on your face!" she laughed.
"The cows didn't answer back."

Solvig Says No Ring-Around-the-Rosy

We murdered fat mosquitoes
  Some bloody nights up there.
More than once we made a smudge
  To smoke our clothes and hair.

I got so sick of porridge,
  Although we had the milk!
They made you sort of nauseous—
  Butter, cream, their ilk.

I'm saying it was sort of hard.
  We weren't just having fun
With ring-around-the-rosy
  And chewing on a bun,

Especially once the mushrooms came,
  For which the cows went mad.
We'd have to hunt the herd for miles
  Then. That was bad.

Of course, we had our coffee.
  We were quick to brew.
So nice to sit there in the shade
  And sip, take in the view.

Sometimes we'd snare a rabbit.
  That made a meaty stew.
But, ish, reconstituted fish?
  You eat it! Pugh!

Lisa Talks of Bedding Down

You know, there comes a kind of gentleness
From work with animals. Oh, sure, there's some
Turn hard and mean from all the muck and mess,
From stubborn creatures they believe are dumb.

But that was rare. I keep thinking of
Those evenings when the cows were bedded down
On moss we had collected, clean and soft.
After supper, we would gather round

The flicker of the fire with our knitting,
Singing songs, or Hedda held us spellbound
With a spooky story, shadows flitting
On the dusky walls. We settled down,

Easy with each other then. I might
Comb out Alva's hair, or Solvig would complain
About her feet, and there in that dim light
One of us would handle them to ease her pain.

Sleep was coming, sleep, our gentle drug.
Our beds were straw, but we had lace and sheets,
Quilts and feather pillows, too, quite snug,
Where we murmured of the men we hoped to meet.

How They Handled Alva's Calf

Alva had the cutest calf
She treated like her special pet.
A cowgirl shouldn't act like that,
But she was just a calf, herself.

Then Sanna fell and broke her leg.
We knew we'd have to slaughter her.
"Waste not, want not" was our motto.
Sobbing, Alva wailed and begged

Me and Solvig if we'd butcher,
She would herd our cows all day.
We took pity, whet our knives,
Killing time till we could watch her

Lead the cattle out of sight.
Solvig drew back Sanna's head.
I cut clean across her throat.
We'd seen this often, did it right.

To make a pudding that we liked,
We placed a pan to catch the blood,
Then strung her up and peeled the hide,
So small it was pathetic.

The jays knew it was time to eat.
Several gathered in the trees,
And they came swooping down
When Solvig held out bits of meat.

We had a fire smoking hot,
And, hungry from the bloody work,
We spit some chunks on alder sticks
To roast, then ate them on the spot.

My, but she was tender! Veal,
I guess a butcher might have said.
She'd made an entertaining pet
But made an even better meal.

Her guts were piled on the ground.
We'd clean her small intestines, too,
But still had lots of meat to dress—
Big job, but no one else around.

Elbow-deep in all this mess,
Our faces sweaty, dark with soot,
We heard this fellow shout, "Hello?"
A man who'd brought supplies to us.

Our arms were smeared with blood and fat.
The shock that showed on that man's face!
He must have wondered what on earth
It was that he was looking at!

Hedda Left Behind

There was this old woman, Hedda,
   Annalisa's mother's aunt,
   Who treated all us girls like friends,
Though she loved nature more than people.

Working at the cow camp every year
   For many summers—sixty-odd—
   Hedda lost her faith in God.
She believed in trees and pasture.

Hedda had a way with cows and goats,
   As if she spoke their language.
   That woman could engage
The smallest birds by whistling their notes.

Talking with you, she'd forget
   Herself and moo, maybe, or growl,
   Or hoot a little, like an owl.
Today, they'd say she had Tourette's.

To us, she just was old Aunt Hedda.
   Hedda smoked a pipe. She told stories.
   Some were sweet, but I preferred them gory.
I can't forget Aunt Hedda, ever.

Once she fell, she came out crooked,
   Yet she still limped up to camp,
   Where she could trim and shine the lamps
And do a little cooking.

Finally she grew so weak
   She simply could not make the trip.
   I heard her family's men drew slips
To choose who'd have to speak.

That year, she stood out in her yard
   To watch us go, holding to a tree.
   I never dreamed I'd have to see
An old one cry so hard.

They Scorn the Warnings

If you played a fantastic fiddle,
You'd slept with the devil.
   That's what the pastor said.

If you sang with great beauty,
You'd learned from the Lady
   Of the Woods, the pastor said.

If you could break hearts with your horn,
Your kids would never be born.
   That's what the pastor said.

But the cows loved us, and the boys loved us
Because we were so dangerous.
   That pastor? He's long dead.

Animal Spirits

On Saturdays, we'd air the rooms
In hopes that, later, boys would come.
We swept the place with leafy brooms
And washed ourselves from hair to bum.

We slipped into our cleanest clothes.
Alva picked some fragrant flowers,
Set them here and there, just so,
And then we'd reach the witching hour.

Voices floated from below,
As men walked up the mountainside,
Singing as they came, so strong and low
They made me kind of ache inside.

It seemed halfway unnatural,
But every group of men fell quiet,
Standing by the cow corral.
They wouldn't come unless invited.

Well, these were Dala men, you know.
They're pretty nice but awful shy.
A little brännvin helped them go,
And later you might find out why

They were so scared of their desire.
We gave them something good to eat,
And soon a fiddler grew inspired
So we all were on our feet.

Oh, those nights of summer dancing
In the cabins! How we flung
Ourselves around! We took chances.
Aren't you meant to when you're young?

Boys from home were nice enough,
But I liked mysteries and riddles,
Men from elsewhere, who would laugh
With me or play a wicked fiddle.

We went in for lots of teasing.
You might mark a man with soot
To say you found him pleasing.
Some boys would blush, and that was sweet.

Sometimes a pair went out of doors,
Toward the woods where moss grew deep.
We knew what they were going for.
It wasn't just to fall asleep!

Well, we were farm girls! We knew life
And had our ways to please a boy
Without a vow to be his wife!
There's such a thing as animal joy.

We'd been warned by older ladies
And some songs that said, "Take care,
The woods are full of crying babies."
Who would want hers buried there?

But those were lovely times and sweet.
Sometimes at night I hear them sing.
The madness of our flying feet!
A fiddle note still lingering.

Helga Tells the Homecoming

When we came off the mountain,
   Oh, we were something then!
They all ran out to greet us—
   Children, women, men.

We'd woven autumn flower crowns
   And stuck them in our hair.
The cows wore decorations, too.
   We wouldn't leave them bare.

The family recognized the bell
   I'd hung on our lead cow,
So they'd come tumbling out and shout:
   "They're here! They're coming now!"

You see, they had to honor you
   For what you had produced,
Such quantities of whey and cheese
   To see the winter through.

You'd hand a tasty chunk of cheese
   To all the little ones
But save the best piece for your beau,
   And you'd go off. What fun!

Well, here I sit in this big chair,
   And everything's a blur,
Though I was pretty, long ago,
   And could I blow the lur!

Old age is full of trouble
  That I can't recommend,
But I was on the mountain once,
  And I was happy then.

Sunday Service at the Cow Camp

Invited to midsommar Sunday service,
We drove into the hills above the lake.
Gladhearted, I was also slightly nervous
Since the pastor'd asked me to participate.

We sat on simple benches, weathered planks,
And mild sunlight beamed a benediction
While the handsome minister gave thanks
And Margit, in her folk dress, read the lesson.

I rose and read those verses out in English.
The congregation sang. The minister
Conveyed a sermon in the gibberish
Of dialect abandoned by my ancestors.

I drifted, blessed by bird song and the buzz
Of insects there among rude buildings where
The custom of the village cowgirls was,
For centuries, to whisper fervent prayer

To random spirits: *Randa, Forest Lady,*
Little People, Fire, Baby Jesus,
Keep the hungry bears and wolves at bay,
And may our cows produce fine cheeses.

The cowgirls buried steel beneath the floors
Of barns and sang away their nightly fear
Of trolls and ghosts, the living dark outdoors.
Wisps of watchful spirits lingered here

As the little congregation sang again.
Silence, then, to which we all were sworn,
Somehow, once the pastor said, "Amen."
And then we heard the music of a horn—

A cow horn played by one we could not see.
My breath came quick. I felt a pleasant chill
And raised my eyes above the rocks and trees
To gaze across the distant, purple hills.

Like a picnic, then, midsommar church
Broke up. People spoke of ordinary life,
And we were led beneath a grand old birch
To meet the pastor's fresh and sexy wife.

Winding down the hill, I asked our hostess
Why Lisa disappeared behind the shed
To blow her horn. "Oh, she's just embarrassed.
She blows so hard her face turns red."

V

Nordic Accordion

In the piney woods of Nisswa,
  In a sun-shot glade, in the middle
Of a rowdy, raucous tune,
  The fiddle drops out,
The bass becomes a heartbeat,
  And Irene Tillung,
All the way from Norway,
  Bends her head, and, resting
Her chin on her accordion,
  Gazes at the buttons
Ranged beneath her hand,
  Fingers pressing this one,
That one, this one,
  Wandering, meandering,
And we stop breathing
  While the origami folds
Of her black accordion
  Inhale the fragrant air
And do our breathing for us.

O, melodious accordion,
  Much maligned, misunderstood
Butt of many jokes—
  That musician in Chicago
Who didn't want to leave
  His accordion in sight
On the back seat of his car,
  But, driven by his hunger,

Went into the restaurant,
    And, coming out, sure enough,
Found his window smashed,
    But nobody had snatched
His accordion, but worse:
    There on the seat, beside
His instrument, there sat
    A second accordion!

O, pitiful, beautiful, portable
    Melodeon, chest-pack organ,
Piano-on-a-strap,
    At last we understand
You're a box full of treasure,
    Opened for our pleasure,
And Irene runs the jewelry
    Through her hands.

And when the music ends,
    We give one collective gasp
Of gratitude for comfort,
    Consolation, life-support.
Applauding and applauding,
    We make a sound like water,
Like an icy mountain stream
    That falls five hundred feet
Into the fjord.

Runes of the North

Birch bark starts. Cedar's fast.
Ash and maple last.

Quick say-so
May not know.

Even those on skis must pee.

Rooms in big houses often stand empty.
Two words to study. They are "good plenty."

Polka, two-step, schottische, waltz.
She won't be impressed by somersaults.

Off-lake winds are wild.
Off-shore leaves a lonely child.

If you've got your big fat head attached,
You won't wear snowshoes to a boxing match.

A simple life has grace. Endure. Observe
The smooth axe handle's curve.

An oar is not a paddle.
The horse goes underneath the saddle.

Thorfinn, Thorkel, and Snorri was here.

Worried looks are allowed.
Even the bear keeps an eye out.

Those people aren't singing;
They're Swedish.

Crows are smarter than you think.
Don't think those birds don't think.

Got himself a snow machine
But wouldn't know a wolf from a wolverine.

In a pinch, an igloo will do
But probably not for you.

Arrowhead Saga

In sagas of the Icelanders,
A reader is struck, sometimes, as if
Whacked in the head by a halberd,
To see so many poets appear:
Hallfred the Troublesome, Bard the Peevish,
Sarcastic Halli, Thorkel the Wise.
Much like today, most of those men
Earned their place in the world with work
Beside their wizardly way with words:
One was a first-rate farmer, another
Was fierce in a fight. Bard the Peevish
Employed his powers part-time.
Once, on a journey with others, they all
Got caught in a storm. Distressed,
His companions obeyed his command,
Held hands in a circle, cried "Ja!"
Altogether, while Bard walked backwards
Around them, muttering Irish. Waving
His white hanky high at the hilltops,
Bard banished the blizzard. Such work
And words were often rewarded with gold
Or horses or swords in those days,
Whereas poor poets in these lean times
Receive no more than free magazines.

Here, in the Arrowhead region, smack
Alongside Lake Superior, resided
Many fine poets, who, in their prime,

Were poorly paid. The least they deserve
Is name-honor now, nor shall we forget
Their grief and good works in the North.
There was a man called Louis the Gloom.
He threw crackling curses at clouds and the cold.
Crank and curmudgeon he was but could cook
And brighten a room with jokes about doom.
Ellie the Eloquent laughed at herself
But composed the most difficult valentines.
Ryan the Vine drank wine, of course:
Nomen *est omen*. Large and ominous,
Vine did not shake his baby because
He had been warned by a nurse. Tender
Big men are attractive; so is their verse.
Junk Store Jane, an old type of writer,
Felt fine refusing newfangledness,
Her poem-hoard piled high in her house.
Jim the Finn was hard to find,
For he was so often lost in the forest
He became Bard of Birch Bark.
Crafty Connie eventually fled
For the far Southwest but left many lines
That seemed to see the insides of things.
Sheila the Red had worked in the mines,
Gone against dragons—The Grinder,
The Winch, the Agglomerator.
Red dust hid in her hair, and some
Still clung to her shoes. In her youth,
She could belt back the beer.
Cooper the Cryer wept nonstop.
Her words were wet, and why not,

Since everything living finds the same fate?
These and dozens of others there were
Who harbored near Lake Superior,
Whose words were birds in the wind;
But names are like leaves in the fall,
And no one can possibly gather them all.
As for those who were honored above,
Goodbye. They are now out of this saga.

For space must remain for Bart the Beloved,
Beautiful Bart, Scatterbrain Bart,
Braveheart Bart, Sutter the Sulk,
Such a pal and so popular with the people
They never tired of calling him names.
He had landed in the Arrowhead
At midlife, half dead, but having been led,
He prospered here, Mighty of Mouth,
Making poems in praise of the people,
Odd as they were, observing the hawks
And filching fish from the flowing streams.
It seemed he had seen this place in a dream,
And when others told tales of their travels,
He said, "I am at home. Here will I dwell."
Scatterbrain made this Arrowhead Saga,
Hoping his arrows would hit their marks.
Comfort and courage he plucked from the place
So peopled with poets, and, lo, although
The weather was not what he always wanted,
He consoled himself on the colder nights
With the warmth of his wife, for whom he was gaga,
Re-reading the old Icelandic sagas.

Forgive Me, Edith Södergran

Oh, Edith Södergran, I've had it hard.
I did not get the place I wanted, felt that I deserved,
And so I worked at pointless jobs for years.
How I suffered. Hurt by women, I
Betrayed them in my turn. So we're the same, then,
Aren't we, Edith Södergran? My mother's dad,
Like you, a Swedish Finn, escaped to this
America, complaining bitterly,
His mother hauling him on by the hand,
And where was her husband then? Nowhere.
There was illness and death in my family. I drank
And made lament, I drank and called some names,
I did, Edith Södergran. I drank, but then,
Finally, at forty, quit. I stopped, although
I still complained. I suffered just insufferably.
Self-pity's so delicious. How could I give it up?

But thanks to you, I can, Edith Södergran,
For, though we are alike, we're clearly not
The same since you're a woman, I'm a man
And aging fast, whereas your lovely body
Died, at thirty-one, of the tuberculosis
That ate your father when you were fifteen.
Once a year I catch a cold. I cough and cough.
The critics called your writing laughable,
While I've won little prizes, Edith Södergran.
War broke down your door. I watch it on TV.
You spooned thin soup and dwindled down.

I devour chicken, lamb, beefsteak, ham,
With dollars in my wallet, dollars in the bank.
You ran out of paper, sold your furniture
And lingerie to go on living, died,
Yet here you are in letters and your poems.

You said your soul was a light blue dress
The color of the sky. I see you on the shore
Of Lake Superior, late in spring, when heaps
Of light blue ice lie shattered on the rocks
And clouds of steam drift off the water.
I see you there, but then you're gone.
I've stopped complaining, Edith Södergran,
So just stand still and wait for me. I'll bring you meat.
I'll bring you writing paper, pen and ink.
My wife and I will welcome you. We have
An extra room. We like the things you like.
Our house has walls of books, and some are Swedish, too.
My wife will help you shop for fancy underthings.
Together, we'll drink tea and just enjoy
The cherry trees when they put on their smocks
Or go out in the woods, as you did as a girl,
To gather wild berries we can share
Or find bloodroot and wood anemone
Or simply stand and breathe the fragrant air.

An Evening of Swedish Folk Songs

There are bony brown cows in this music,
Mugs of hot milk spiced with pepper.
The last few asters of autumn are here,
The first flickering flakes of snow.
Moonlight is trapped in these tunes,
The cries of white-haired women,
And the wind sneaks in beneath the door.
Here is the breadknife my sister stuck
      in the landlord's guts,
A Bible, a candle, and a birchbark bowl
In the low-slung hut made of sod and sticks
Where I lived six hundred years ago.

Acknowledgments

I am grateful to the editors of the following magazines and anthologies in which some of these poems, or earlier versions of them, first appeared:

The Freshwater Review: "A Taste for Ptarmigan"

Great River Review: "What Swedes Eat"

Lost Lake Folk Opera: "I Come from Quiet People," "Strange Doings at Ross Elementary, 1956"

Nodin Poetry Anthology: "Tussocks"

North Coast Review: "An Evening of Swedish Folk Songs"

Ovenbird Poetry (On-line): "Dagna Fahlstrom Fails to Send a Postcard Home," "The Immigrants: A Story by Tom Mc-Grath"

A Poetry Congeries (On-line): "A Nice Little Tavern in the Woods," "Tussocks"

The Raintown Review: "Funeral Rites"

The Rotary Dial (On-line): "Birgit and Guri," "Halvor Halvorson," "Runes of the North"

Slant: "What Happened up in Uppsala"

Stoneboat: "On Being Mistaken for Dan Carlson"

Valparaiso Review (On-line): "First Night on Sollerön," "Grand Casino"

Whistling Shade: "Forgive Me, Edith Södergran"

All but one of the poems in Section IV are included in *Cow Calls in Dalarna,* a chapbook published by Scott King's Red Dragonfly Press in June of 2016. All of the poems in Section IV are included in *Cow Calls in Dalarna: A Readers' Theatre Play in Verse with Folk Music,* directed by Sheryl Jensen and premiered at the Midsommar Fest sponsored by the Swedish Cultural Society of Duluth in June of 2016 with funding support from the Lloyd K. Johnson Foundation and the Swedish Council of America. Additional performances followed in July of that year at the American Swedish Institute in Minneapolis.

"The Immigrants: A Story by Tom McGrath" is an enhanced version of a teaching story I heard the late Thomas McGrath tell in public twice. He also told a version of this story in *The Movie at the End of the World,* a documentary film by Mike Hazard. McGrath never made a poem of this story, but I've found it so helpful I thought that someone should, so I put it in blank verse.

"Wheelbarrow Man" is based on a brief account in *Encounter on the Great Plains: Scandinavian Settlers and the Dispossession of Dakota Indians, 1890 – 1930* by Karen V. Hansen. I transposed the story from the voice of a professional historian into oral history told in the local vernacular.

"Mina Anderson Contradicts the Author Vilhelm Moberg" is a first-person, blank verse summary of the life of that immigrant woman based on the historical study *I Go to America: Swedish American Women and the Life of Mina Anderson* by Joy K. Lintelman.

The poem relies both on excerpts from Anderson's own writing, which are fundamental to the book, and Lintelman's investigation of the broader experience of Swedish American immigrant women.

"A Nice Little Tavern in the Woods" is based on local lore in north central Minnesota as conveyed to me by my friend Jack Hickerson.

"Halvor Halvorson" is historical fiction. I came across a brief, informal biographical account while staying in a rental cabin near Lutsen, Minnesota, and, after a few years, while my imagination worked on what I remembered of the story, this poem emerged.

The cycle of poems in Section IV was inspired by visits to the summer pasture camps of Sweden, chiefly Flenarna in Dalarna, over a quarter of a century. I am deeply grateful to the folks who arranged those visits, explaining things and telling stories. My interest was also quickened and informed by Swedish books and entries on the web. I'm especially grateful, however, to Kerstin Brorson for her evocative study, *Sing the Cows Home: The Remarkable Herdswomen of Sweden.*

Nordic Accordion is dedicated to my brother Ross, who has made his living by singing the old songs of Scandinavia, America, Ireland, and Scotland. For more than thirty years, I've had the joy and privilege of pairing up with him as The Sutter Brothers, a poetry-and-music duo, performing at community art centers, universities, libraries, and other venues. I don't know how any poet could stand next to Ross as he sings a ballad that's four hundred years old, witness its effect on the audience, and not be tempted to try traditional forms. My brother's influence is everywhere in this book.

My thanks, also, to Ross' wife, Mary Lofgren, for not only tolerating but applauding my work with him, for canny suggestions, and for countless acts of hospitality.

Cheryl Dannenbring, Jim Johnson, Milan Kovacovic, Angela Leuck, Steve Luxton, Ilze Mueller, Walt Prentice, Jane and Doran Whitledge, Pat and Laurie Wilson, and the late Phil Dacey read and listened, offering suggestions and encouragement.

Thanks to Bill and Margareta Beyer, Joe and Lyn Muldoon, and Carol Westberg for sustained interest over the years. Bill and Margareta went so far as to translate several poems for my readings in Sweden. I continue to be dumbfounded by Jean Replinger's friendship and financial support.

Thanks to my daughters and their partners for their long-suffering, appreciation, and friendship.

Endless gratitude to my wife, Dorothea Diver, for patience and belief, encouragement and critiques, for playing Swedish folk tunes on piano, and for her enthusiastic interest in Scandinavian language and culture, even though she's highly Irish.

– Bart Sutter

photo: Shawna Vine

About the Author

Bart Sutter received the Minnesota Book Award for poetry with *The Book of Names: New and Selected Poems*, for fiction with *My Father's War and Other Stories*, and for creative non-fiction with *Cold Comfort: Life at the Top of the Map*. Among other honors, he has won a Jerome Foundation Travel & Study Grant (Sweden), a Loft-McKnight Award, and the Bassine Citation from the Academy of American Poets. In 2006, he was named the first Poet Laureate of Duluth. He has written for public radio, he has had four verse plays produced, and he often performs as one half of The Sutter Brothers, a poetry-and-music duo. Bart Sutter lives on a hillside overlooking Lake Superior with his wife, Dorothea Diver.